TEN YEARS OF DESIGN EXCELLENCE
CERAMIC TILES OF ITALY ACROSS AMERICA

TEN YEARS
OF DESIGN
EXCELLENCE
CERAMIC TILES
OF ITALY
ACROSS AMERICA

Text by Jen Renzi

For a complete list of Ceramic Tiles of
Italy Publications, please visit
www.italiatiles.com.

First published in the United States of
America by Edizioni Press, Inc. 469 West
21st Street New York, New York 10011
www.edizionipress.com

ISBN: 1-931536-39-2

Library of Congress Catalogue Card
Number: 2004101088

Project Supervisor: Luciano Galassini

Editor: Christine Abbate,
Novitá Communication

Design: Giona Maiarelli, maiarelli studio

Printed and bound by Mondadori,
Verona, Italy

Special thanks to the Italian Trade
Commission for their collaboration on
this project. The Ceramic Tile
Department of the Italian Trade
Commission can be reached at
33 E 67th Street, New York, NY 10021
or www.italytile.com.

Ceramic Tiles of Italy

This publication is sponsored by
Ceramic Tiles of Italy, a trademark
of Assopiastrelle - the Association of
Italian Ceramic Tile and Refractory
Manufacturers

Good design of all stripes—whether traditional or modern, refined or radical—depends on vision. It relies on inspired ideas and the ingenuity and appropriateness of their execution—aesthetically, mechanically, economically, ecologically. Inimical to the design process is a degree of compromise. Architects and designers begin with an ideal, and then search for methods and materials to realize that ideal. Limitations of budget and structure, unfortunately, present themselves even before pencil is set to paper. Compromise is often unavoidable.

Not so with ceramic tile, which artfully reconciles form and function. It is one of the most economical surfacing options, particularly when taking into account the material's easy installation and maintenance, as well as its wearability over time. Functionally, it is virtually unsurpassed. Incredibly durable, it can withstand extreme environmental conditions, from harsh weather to corrosive chemicals. Composed of natural, sustainable raw materials, and increasingly formed by ecologically sound production processes, ceramic tile is also an eco-friendly alternative to other surfacing materials and decorative finishes.

Apart from these many attributes, ceramic tile is also aesthetically diverse. It's offered in limitless colors, textures, finishes, shapes, sizes, and looks, lending it a chameleon-like personality. Large-format slabs of matte porcelain tile with a stone-like finish impart a decidedly different feel from a wall of glossy red glazed mosaics or an exterior courtyard of rough-hewn pavers. No matter the idiom a designer aspires to—formal, edgy, rustic—or the particular program or application in question, there exists a ceramic tile option to answer those needs. Not just a practical choice, ceramic tile is a vehicle for upholding design vision.

To an ever-increasing degree, designers are turning to Italian manufacturers for the best and most exciting product. Italy accounts for 36% of the international trade of ceramic tile and for 27% of the U.S. market—the world's largest. These impressive figures attest to the technical and aesthetic superiority of the country's output, and to the industry's collective, unwavering commitment to progress and innovation. Architects and designers worldwide are quick to trumpet the many benefits of sourcing Italian ceramic tile. Richness of coloration. The highest standards of quality. Unparalleled variety. A pledge to ecologically sound production methods. And peerless artistry, particularly when it comes to parroting in form—and surpassing in function—other natural materials like marble, limestone, and even metal.

From furniture to architecture to automobiles, the ascendancy of Italian design throughout history is rooted in canny, even visionary collaborations between manufacturers and designers—a dovetailing of business and art. Makers of ceramic tile are a part of this illustrious tradition. The Italian industry has emerged as a world leader by anticipating what customers need to affect good design—be it enhanced functionality or particular decorative features—and quick to develop and introduce these products into the marketplace.

Ceramic Tiles of Italy has been a guiding force in fostering a dialogue between its 241 member manufacturers and the American design community, thanks in large part to its prestigious awards program. Launched a decade ago, the competition lauds notable, innovative use of tile in commercial and residential applications throughout the U.S., spanning all project types and every mode of expression from traditional to contemporary. The competition's development charts what has happened in the industry—in particular, an explosive demand for product and tremendous ingenuity in how the material is used. Ten years after its inception, the design competition, developed in cooperation with the Italian Trade Commission, has matured to an annual competition, with a codified series of guidelines, and draws submissions from every corner of the nation.

In addition to heralding creativity, the program has allowed Ceramic Tiles of Italy to research and stay abreast of marketplace trends. Recent developments include the increasing popularity of ceramic tile as exterior cladding—a role the material is well suited to given its low porosity and its resistance to fading, scratching, frost, and humidity. Long used on building exteriors throughout Europe, it is starting to gain favor here as a practical and affordable alternative that encourages design-forward statements; witness Richard Fleischman's inspired and inspiring design for the

Head Start Facility, a publicly funded elementary school in downtown Cleveland, OH. Large-format tiles—bigger than 12 inches square—are popular as well, particularly in corporate interiors where ceramic rivals marble and other stones as the embodiment of luxury and professionalism. Swanke Hayden Connell's deployment of a similar tile variety in two very different workplace interiors—one soothing and stately, the other industrial and urbane—is evidence of the material's flexibility and appropriateness for a range of applications. In hospitality and residential settings, where ceramic tile's durability and functionalism has long been coveted, inventive use of the material is proliferating. Once sourced primarily for bathrooms, kitchens, and other wet areas, ceramic tile is coming to its own as a means for conjuring a specific mood.

The occasion of the competition's 10-year anniversary inspired this volume, conceived as a source book of ideas and applications. The projects surveyed, selected from Ceramic Tiles of Italy Design Competition winners, span project types, scales, geographic location, mood, spirit, and aesthetic. This book demonstrates Italian ceramic tile's dexterity, its breath of offerings, its suitability to a wealth of applications, and its ability to match the unlimited ideas designers dream up.

While commemorating a mere ten years of excellent, creative use of this ancient building material, this book also prefigures advancements to come. Ceramic tile's most elemental function is to define and draw boundaries—walls, floors, ceilings, zones, surfaces, borders, frames. The designer's role is to keep breaking boundaries, to always look ahead.

Ceramic Tiles of Italy
Design Competition
Recent ads

01_SPORTS & RECREATION

From sports clubs to natatoriums, facilities devoted to physical fitness receive a punishing workout on a daily basis. Even athletes take down time to recuperate—not so gymnasiums and fitness centers, which are often open seven days a week, morning to night. Constant foot traffic, dropped exercise equipment, chlorinated puddles, and harsh cleaning chemicals are just some of the antagonists a designer must account for in selecting building materials and finishes.

And image, moreover, is everything. A university gym is a three-dimensional platform for communicating school spirit and team prowess. For health clubs, establishing or reinforcing brand identity is a crucial factor in competing for clientele. The design also needs to address state of mind as well as body, bolstering energy or perhaps instilling a relaxing, spa-like ambiance.

For sports and recreation applications, ceramic tile's durability, easy maintenance, resistance to moisture, and variety of decorative options prove a particularly winning combination.

MOJO STUMER
EQUINOX HEALTH CLUB

For work-out enthusiasts, the body is a temple—and the gym no less than a multitasking community center. We expect a lot of our health clubs. What was once a hum-drum, utilitarian place to hoist a few free weights, in our fitness-obsessed age, has become a locus for specialized activities from tai chi to cardio-funk. To say nothing of a hub for networking, web surfing, and even receiving spa treatments.

Mojo Stumer + Associates has designed seven such facilities for the upscale Equinox chain in New York and Los Angeles. Although ceramic tile has featured prominently in all, the Second Avenue location in Manhattan provided an opportunity to push the material further. "In the past, we'd mostly relegated tile to locker rooms," explains principal Mark Stumer. "Here, we used it as a major design feature in the public areas as well. It's a beautiful material—we wanted to take it beyond the work areas and use it more decoratively."

Numerous varieties animate floors and accent walls throughout the 30,000-square-foot space, which extends three levels underground and includes a 17-yard pool. Stumer considered other surfacing materials, but concluded that ceramic tile would best help him achieve a forward-thinking design that could withstand the tremendous wear-and-tear the space receives on a continual basis. Shifting styles, colors, shapes, finishes, and patterns influence energy levels and mood. Rough-hewn porcelain tiles from Impronta-Italgraniti, reminiscent of limestone, strike a luxurious note in the lobby. Spirited high-gloss tiles of yellow and bold blue in corridors and the pool area remedy dark windowless conditions. Near the reception, a wall of shimmery grey Bisazza mosaics form a chic backdrop to recessed stainless-steel niches displaying Equinox's product line. "Ceramic tile helped us achieve the design we'd sold the client on, juxtaposing slick and rough materials," says Stumer.

WADDELL & ASSOCIATES
CLEVELAND STATE UNIVERSITY LOCKER ROOM

A superior sports program requires more than just a great coach, skilled players, and a winning attitude—state-of-the-art athletic facilities are just as critical to success. To get a leg up on the competition, Cleveland State University enlisted Waddell & Associates Architects to overhaul the men's locker room of its gymnasium. The uninviting 1970s-era facility was distinguished by exposed concrete-block walls and dank, claustrophobic conditions that partner Mark Waddell describes as dehumanizing—a major deterrent for both recruitment purposes and for school pride. "This facility is used and seen by a lot of people. The design needed to reflect the university's overall goals, communicating that Cleveland State is a very current, happening place," says Waddell. "Student recruitment and retainment is so competitive these days—everything has to be leading-edge."

Flooring and wall coverings, continues Waddell, were both places to make a major design statement. He lined almost every available surface with porcelain tiles from Caesar Ceramiche; the material's unparalleled durability and moisture resistance helped him to create design statements strong enough both visually and structurally to withstand the abuse of college students. Wall tiles are high-gloss, floor tiles have a slip-resistant matte finish—an important consideration given that the adjacent pool leads to very wet conditions. Waddell exploited the difference in finish as a decorative feature: "The subtle nuances read so well in ceramic tile."

Broad strokes of colored tile wend through a neutral background, pulling users through circulation routes and creating a sense of vibrancy in the subterannean, windowless space. Waddell chose Italian tile for its unparalleled variety. "I was drawn to the range and richness of color available," he explains. "As a designer, you get a very specific idea in your head, and commit to searching high and low for the right products to fit that criteria."

02_RETAIL

With a ceramic tile floor, it's okay to shop until you drop. Literally. The material can withstand the impact of flames, heavy machinery, and corrosive chemicals—let alone merchandise-laden shoppers collapsing from exhaustion.

A modern interpretation of the bustling urban bazaar, shopping centers are cityscapes in miniature. Or not so miniature, in the case of vast suburban malls that may extend for tens of millions of square feet. Encompassing cinemateques, restaurants, recreation areas, and other family-oriented amenities, today's retail environments are all-day destinations designed to accommodate every mode of consumption: shopping, eating, and entertainment.

Capable of toughing it out against the physical rigors of commerce, ceramic tile is an easy sell for mass-market malls. Thanks to its refined beauty, it's also a perfect fit for exclusive, upscale boutiques.

And talk about retail therapy: Italian ceramic tile comes in enough colors, finishes, textures, glazes, patterns, sizes, and shapes to please even the most discerning customer—or devoted shopoholic.

KA ARCHITECTURE
RIVERTOWN CROSSING

A mid-level mall in suburban Grandville, Michigan, Rivertown Crossing houses six anchor tenants, a 20-screen cinema, 113 stores, and an 850-seat food court. The design scheme is similarly ambitious in scope, weaving nautical elements—a nod to the nearby Great Lakes—throughout the 1.3 million-square-foot complex. Trusses recalling interlaced bridgework punctuate the main concourse. Glass handrails along the second-story bridge are fritted with a wave motif. An exterior stair tower takes the form of a bright-blue lighthouse—the mall's logo—an image that reappears on seating and tables.

The most dramatic interpretation of the theme is the food court floor, a lively patchwork of nautical flags played out in colorful matte-finished Casalgrande-Padana tiles. "Ceramic tile features prominently throughout the project, but we wanted to take it to another level here, since it's such a visible area," says design architect Christine Zakrajsek.

Tile of a more neutral coloration sluices like a river throughout the concourses. A high-gloss finish lends a touch of upscale luxe. Thankfully, no compass or nautical map is needed to locate escalators: a checkerboard floor abets way-finding, even during crowded conditions. "The patterning denotes the major circulation areas, signaling what's happening as patrons approach the center court," says Zakrajsek.

To keep down costs, the designers limited the use of laser-cut tiles in favor of pre-existing designs from the manufacturer's line—bold overscaled geometrics, tartan stripes, loosely arcing lines. "We saved intricate detailing for center court areas, where the floor is visible from second-story overlooks," says Zakrajsek. "There, geometric small-cut tiles create a sort of design-within-a-design." Ceramic tile borders even define break-out spaces within circulation, framing carpeted soft-seating areas.

Vertical surfaces are also treated to tile: tile surfaces bathroom walls, clads neutral pier areas between tenants, and appears as concourse wainscotting near minor entrances.

KA ARCHITECTS
PARKWAY PLACE

To bring down-home southern charm to a down-at-the-heels mall in Huntsville, Alabama, KA Architects took cues from residential design. "It was a complete tear-down, totally lacking in character," says senior design architect Jeffrey Hoskin of the Parkway Place Mall. "But it was relatively small—630,000 square feet—and had a nice rhythm and flow to it. We decided to recast the public areas by reorganizing them into traditionally inspired 'rooms,' each featuring a unique character."

Creating a continuous experience from room to room are sweeping curves: graceful arches, ornamental ironwork, vaulted ceilings, and rounded bulkheads—as well as a fanciful porcelain-tile floor embellished by curvilinear forms. "Because tenants control the storefront elevation in retail environments, the design inevitably centers on the floor and ceiling—and how the two respond to one another," explains Hoskin.

The designers repeated patterns and imagery in different sizes to address shifts in volume and scale throughout. An abstracted scroll motif, which accents wainscoting at entry points, recurs as oversize laser-cut insets in the soaring double-height center courts. Checkerboard patterning also reappears, formed from single or ganged tiles depending on location. Even the mall logo—two offset squares—recurs as tile insets. "We blew it up and shrank it down to help unify the space," says Hoskin.

Vertical surfaces on elevator banks and customer service stations are also clad in tile, stone-like neutral fields scored by dark bands. "Black tile accents let the eye terminate at the edge of walls or floors or patterns," explains Hoskin. "It provides contrast within the natural palette of terra cottas, greens, and warm greys."

The extensive use of porcelain tile by Atlas Concorde and Mirage —which also surfaces restrooms—allowed the architects to make a grand statement that knits the entire space together, ensuring a seamless décor and desirable price point. "We were able to get the upscale look of stone at a much lower cost," concludes Hoskin.

ANTHONY BELLUSCHI
STRATFORD SQUARE MALL

Like hip handbags or funky footwear, even the most fashion-forward shopping center has a shelf life. Witness the Stratford Square Mall in Bloomingdale, Illinois. "It was a staple in the community, but it began to look extremely dated," explains principal Mike Patrick Sullivan. Hired to enact a much-needed makeover, the designers played up the mall's one salvageable asset. "It featured an extensive skylight system, inspiring us to recast the interior public areas as outdoor space and create a series of garden-themed elements."

Freshened-up courts and concourses now feature actual landscaping, ivy-covered trellises, seating reminiscent of wrought-iron patio furniture, and an extensive tile program that creates the feeling of a terrace. Large-format modular porcelain tiles from Mirage are installed with Mapei material in a running-bond pattern akin to brick. In the main court, tile takes on a basket-weave appearance. "We even found tiles to mimic stone pavers," Sullivan describes. "Actual stone was considered, but the range of options is much wider with tile, and there are varieties that act very convincingly like stone. The Italian manufacturers offered the best variety of high-quality paving tile."

The installation's relaxed orthogonality was modeled on a European courtyard. "Strong geometry focuses the eye in the big event areas, calling attention to those spots within the sequence of spaces," says Sullivan. "We used softer patterning in between." Graphics are boldest in the center court, the mall's social hub, featuring a low circular fountain that would be at home in an urban plaza. Two secondary break-out courts entertain young shoppers with interactive nature-themed sculptures that spring to life at the touch of a button. Tile continues in the generous family restroom area—ceramic on the walls, porcelain on floors—appointed with residential-style upholstered seating and artwork.

One feature is sure to never go out of style: near the food court, a 50-foot-long wall is covered in 6-inch square ceramic tiles designed by local kids. You're never too young, after all, to appreciate tile's many merits.

TVS
HARBOR ISLAND

Mixed-use facilities demand careful choreography between diverse—and often divergent—needs, expectations, and customer bases. Such was the challenge faced by TVS, hired to breathe new life into a Tampa mall complex encompassing ground-floor retail space and offices above. "It was a little ahead of its time, integrating entertainment, living, and retail under one roof," says senior designer Donna Childs. Interiors, however, had unfortunately fallen a little behind the times. The new look needed to appeal to a range of customers: white-collar office workers, an upscale local crowd, and tourists visiting the neighboring convention center and aquarium. "We wanted to avoid theming, which we thought would alienate the base markets," says principal Tom Porter. Instead, the firm opted for a refined, timeless scheme that reflects the site's proximity to the waterfront. The result is a spatial symphony of fluid lines that excites wayward tourists, impresses business clients, and satisfies neighbors.

Inventive flooring from Pastorelli, Cooperativa Ceramica d'Imola and Ceramica Vogue takes much of the credit for the design's success. A freeflowing mosaic—a collage of five ceramic tile varieties broken and laid by hand—winds through all public areas. Defining traffic flow, the mosaic cuts a swath through a grid of beige ceramic tiles evocative of stained concrete. "We got the same look by using porcelain tile, but without the maintenance issues," claims Childs. The mosaic treatment also continues along baseboards near escalators and other key public areas.

Tile appears on walls and floors in restrooms, where soothing earth tones and animated borders inject a sense of warmth. "Using porcelain tile in restrooms is really a no-brainer," says Childs. "It's excellent in terms of slip resistance—and you can guarantee a mall floor is going to be wet!"

The result is a comfortable space that encourages lingering—and sales. "We've done a number of exit studies, and what people remember most in retail environments is the floor," explains Porter. "It's a critical component that can leave a lasting, positive impression—flooring is the single element shoppers stay in contact with throughout their experience."

03_CONTRACT

Most of us spend as much—if not more—time in our offices as we do in our homes. Not a comforting thought. Thankfully, employers from Silicon Valley to Wall Street, ad firms to law firms, recognize to an increasing degree the impact of a well-designed office on staff morale, communication, productivity, and even creativity. The hierarchical cube-farm paradigm is falling from favor as employers loosen their ties and embrace freedom, flexibility, and individual needs in the workplace.

Corporate offices, at their most inspired, act as three-dimensional brochures, a competitive sales tool to attract both employees and clients. Architectural elements and finishes, particularly in public spaces like lobbies, corridors, cafeterias, and conference areas, are vehicles for expressing the brand. Whether innovative or traditional, corporations want to signify professionalism, authority, and trustworthiness. All values that ceramic tile—a workhorse in the workplace—upholds.

SWANKE HAYDEN CONNELL
REUTERS

For media conglomerate Reuters, relocating to new Times Square headquarters provided an opportunity to consolidate 20 regional offices and a recently acquired subsidiary, Instanet, under one roof. The client requested a forward-thinking scheme that would speak to the firm's industry leadership. "Reuters is about hard-core news—it's not about pretty finishes," explains senior designer Agatha Habjan. "We aimed for an industrial look."

The designers were challenged with creating cohesion throughout 22 levels of office space while accounting for differentiation between Reuters and Instanet floors. "Because the companies had separate identities, we wanted a design element to link the space vertically," says Habjan. Separate color palettes—blue for Reuters, red for Instanet—signal your location. Your first experience on each floor, however, is the floor itself: all elevator lobbies are surfaced in Caesar Ceramica matte-finish tile in a slate-like charcoal hue. For further continuity, the same tile surfaces a much-used third-floor break-out area wrapped in a curved, canted enclosure of backlit acrylic.

The 30th-floor executive conference area presented a different set of conditions. "We used a lot of color on the office floors to reference the Times Square location, but for here we chose a neutral palette," says Habjan. It was important that the corporate identity not be evident, since Reuters rents out this space to other companies. Flooring is a buttery Caesar Ceramica tile that takes on the appearance of limestone. The treatment flows from reception into a perimeter gallery that leads to conference and media rooms. "It's like a sidewalk," Habjan describes. "We took an almost urban approach to the floor." On the opposite side of the floorplate, the tile meanders into a piazza-like area that opens onto prefunction, servery and cafeteria, and private dining rooms.

The clean-lined industrial look dovetails with the client's aesthetic as well as economic goals. "It was a budget-conscious project, so expensive materials were off-limits," says Habjan. "With tile, we got the look of stone, but much greater durability and much lower maintenance."

SWANKE HAYDEN CONNELL
INVESTMENT FIRM OFFICE

When its World Financial Center office was destroyed on 9/11, an investment firm faced an agonizing decision: relocate, or stay put and contend with extensive water damage, toxic debris, to say nothing of psychic baggage. The decision to sensitively overhaul the two-story, 150,000-square-foot office was an admirable commitment to downtown Manhattan—and to the staff. "The client was proud that they were staying, and wanted to acknowledge what happened there with a scheme that made employees feel welcome and safe," explains junior designer Becky Button.

Warm natural materials and soothing earth tones chart a restful, embracing feel. Casalgrande-Padana floor tile in a pale-blonde hue goes a long way to imparting serenity. The tile wends from the elevator lobby through the foyer and main circulation. To negotiate an angular floorplan, the 12-by-18-inch tiles were installed horizontally in an ashlar pattern that seems to weave a diagonal course; the continuous swath underfoot softens the awkward layout. The material also continues up a floating central staircase designed to foster staff interaction.

"The tile chosen was well-priced and is durable, beautiful, and imitative of limestone," says Button. "Because of the fast-track program—we had only 9 months to complete the project—we selected a material we had worked with previously. In addition to its great beauty, Casalgrande-Padana has a fast lead time and was available with a bullnosing, so we could use the same material for the floor and stair treads."

Ceramic tile flooring reappears in the servery, enhanced by other natural materials: celadon glass wall tile, acrylic accent panels embedded with grass, clusters of riverstones below glass countertops. During renovation, the seating area was relocated from a window wall with Hudson River views to one overlooking Ground Zero. Says Button, "The client wanted it to become a place of communal reflection"—and, consequently, communal healing.

ARQUITECTONICA
ARQUITECTONICA STUDIOS

Miami Beach is a city of extremes, a synthesis of conflicting sensibilities. Relentlessly urban yet bordered by miles of luminous beach. Soulful yet sybaritic. Enamored of newness yet tethered to a rich architectural heritage.

To live and work there is to embrace such contrasts with open arms. Which is precisely the approach Arquitectonica's Laurinda Spear and Bernardo Fort-Brescia took in designing a building to house their own offices. The boxy five-story structure—which made a star turn in the film The Birdcage—yokes clean-lined Bauhaus rationalism to exuberant art-deco. Clad in white stucco, the building is encircled by wraparound strip windows, lending the appearance of a seven layer cake. The fenestration is punctuated at random intervals with colorful squares of mosaic tile, in graphic patterning that derives from local Seminole Indian motifs. "The imagery is ubiquitous throughout south Florida," explains Spear. Ceramic tile from Ceramica Vogue adds joie d'vivre—as well as functionality—to the bureau moderne. "We knew from the outset that we wanted to use tile for the exterior," says Spear. "It's impervious to weather, requires almost no maintenance, and the colors don't fade over time." All important considerations for the sun-drenched and hurricane-prone locale.

Piercing one end of the building is a stair and elevator core, stained light-blue to match the cloudless sky. The vertical spine is detailed on three sides with whimsical flourishes—meant to recall the lapping ocean waves—rendered in mosaics of broken tile. Along the streetfront, the shapes punch through the wall to form windows, filtering light and breeze into the stairwell. The designers meshed indoors and out in another way as well: In the ground-floor elevator lobby, doors are bordered in colorful bands of broken tiles—remnants from the exterior detailing.

04_RESIDENTIAL

Residential projects are a microcosm of all the demands that building materials need address: withstanding foot traffic in public areas, offering safety and slip resistance in wet ones, boasting hygienic properties for cooking and eating areas, conveying warmth and comfort in living rooms.

Easy to clean and maintain, ceramic tile is an obvious choice for residential kitchens and bathrooms. It's also at home making a design statement in living areas, as a decorative frieze in a bedroom, as honed slabs for a dining-room floor, or as an accent wall in a den. Offered in virtually limitless shapes, colors, patterns, textures, and finishes, the material suits traditional and progressive decors alike.

To an increasing degree, residential clients are embracing new paradigms of living—from open-plan loft spaces to rooms that perform multiple functions. In kitchens, the social hub of the home, cooking often takes a back seat to entertainment. And bathrooms aren't just about primping in privacy; these days, baths are often conceived as spa-like retreats. Spaces that perform double duties demand building materials that gracefully do the same.

MICHAEL P. JOHNSON DESIGN
YODER HOUSE

Architect Michael Johnson's airy modern home for an Arizona couple is a perfect demonstration of ceramic tile's dual strength—the material's singular ability to bridge function and beauty. Perched on a sloping one-acre site overlooking downtown Phoenix and the nearby Camelback Mountains, the two-story house embraces the outdoors with full-height windows, almost 3,000 square feet of patio space, and a seamless swath of tile flooring that wends from the lower-level car court into the elevator, and continues upstairs through the open-plan living room and contiguous patio cantilevering out to the horizon.

"The scheme required a hard-surface material that would work in all three zones—entry, living area, and patio," says Johnson. "I wanted one product that could deal with all the design issues that entailed." He chose a single variety of tile that functions equally well indoors and out, in public and private areas, by communicating utility and luxury: 12-inch squares of Ceramica Ligure Vaccari's full-bodied porcelain tile with a raised-dot pattern in a honed finish. "Using one surface material makes the space seem much larger visually, smoothing over the transition between levels," says Johnson.

The material stands up to the elements—harsh desert wind and searing sun—as well as the decorative demands of clients Richard Yoder and Jeannie Doorbos. "Tile performs marvelously in wet areas like the garage, laundry, and pool—which require a no-slip surface. It also works with the clients' modern art collection, which is heavy on primary colors." The inky, obsidian swath underfoot also integrates with the structure's steel framework and endless black glass.

"I selected ceramic tile for its function and beauty, but also for its low cost—we sourced almost 10,000 square feet of it," explains Johnson. "I didn't even consider another flooring material. Tile made sense holistically and instinctually."

05_EDUCATION

School campuses—whether facilities for pre-schoolers or post-grads—are a study in the finer points of human growth and development. Perhaps no other building type places such equally rigorous demand on both the design's physical and psychological performance.

Schools must contain and support diverse activities ranging from contemplative individual study to boisterous group activities. Classrooms, auditoriums, cafeterias, and gymnasiums each have distinct spatial and material requirements that architects must consider. Moreover, the design of education facilities must address students' psychological and emotional well-being, providing a comfortable, nurturing, and, above all, safe environment to encourage the learning process and spark an excitement in intellectual inquiry.

Institutions of higher learning require high-style, high-performance building materials. Ceramic tile passes the test—and earns extra credit to boot—thanks to its strength, affordability, and suitability to applications from restrooms to cafeterias to public areas.

RICHARD FLEISCHMAN+PARTNERS
HEAD START FACILITY

A federally funded elementary school for inner-city students in East Cleveland, the Head Start campus unfurls in a series of bold geometric volumes around a grassy central courtyard. Tucked under an arcing roof that swoops up to meet the sky, the low-slung U-shaped building is clad entirely in 8- and 12-inch-square ceramic tiles from Cercom in broad stripes of bright white, warm grey, and sunny yellow.

Architect Richard Fleischman conceived the bright and cheery design to spark a sense of discovery, making kids excited and motivated to come to school. "A building is like a book," he explains. "You want the cover to be as tantalizing and inviting as the content to draw people in."

Literature wasn't Fleischman's only inspiration—art plays a part as well. "I'm drawn to colors that are symbolic, rather than realistic or simply cosmetic. The way Modigliani used reds, for instance, communicates the human spirit, a person's heart and soul." Fleischman chose Italian ceramic tile for its intense and unparalleled coloration. Plus, the material's inherent resistance to fading and weathering ensures that the bright hues won't lose their luster over time.

On a pragmatic level, the building's extensive glazing and perimeter circulation routes draw a fluid boundary between inside and out—meaning the exterior is always visible from within. The choice of tile on the exterior allowed Fleischman to make a dramatic, large-scale statement within tight budgetary constraints.

The Head Start facility gets an A+ in fine art, as well as economics: "Schools need to communicate the beauty and purpose of learning," says Fleischman, who is quick to find poetry in the utilitarian. "Math teaches students to think logically. Language class teaches students culture. And art teaches passion." In this case, a passion for learning.

06_HEALTHCARE

Designers of medical facilities face daunting obstacles. Very few surfacing materials and finishes offer the necessary resistance to germs, pathogens, and the chemicals used to eradicate them. In treatment areas, function must be prioritized over form, and specialized equipment often dictates spatial flow, leaving little room for creativity.

Just as imperative is addressing the human spirit—usually at its most fragile when medical matters are at hand. Uplifting surroundings can enhance the healing process by restoring dignity, reconnecting patients and loved ones back to their everyday lives, and alleviating the stress and anxiety inherent to receiving medical treatment.

Equal parts high-tech and high-touch, ceramic tile's structural composition renders it one of the most hygienic options for health-care facilities. Impervious to liquids and resistant to contaminants, it's easily disinfected. It marries slip resistance and cleanability to an unprecedented degree, ensuring physical safety. Chemically inert, it's also a non-toxic, eco-friendly alternative to vinyl—healthy for the environment as well as healing bodies.

HEMMLER & CAMAYD
O'NEILL CENTER
FOR HEALTHY FAMILIES

Eastern and western medicine may differ in spirit and methodology, but both traditions agree that peak health depends on a link between mind and body, interior and exterior. The O'Neill Center for Healthy Families, a community-oriented facility in Scranton, Pennsylvania, promotes wellness through academic study, preventative-care programs, eastern-influenced offerings like yoga and meditation—and a design that likewise achieves holism between inside and out. Nestled in a woodsy grove of oak and maple trees on Marywood University's campus, the facility houses classrooms as well as the school's nutrition department, a women's clinic, and a human-performance laboratory. The heart and soul of the building is a sunlit double-height atrium, a central hub that forms a pivot point between two masonry wings. A perfect cube with soaring glass curtain walls, the space exhibits a strong visual connection with the great outdoors. "The atrium reflects an ethereal, meditative quality, while exposing and expressing the building's steel structure," explains partner John Kuna.

Decorative touches and material choices reinforce the strong tie to nature. Structural columns of Paralam sprout like abstracted trees in every corner. A catwalk connecting the two wings at the second-floor level is surfaced with wood slats. And lush ceramic tile flooring flows from the atrium into adjacent waiting areas and restrooms, where it also surfaces walls. The designers selected a Magica honed-finish tile in an earthy greenish-grey hue, designed to mimic the tone and texture of a flagstone patio. Selected in various sizes—12-inch squares, 6-inch squares, and 12-by-6-inch rectangles—the tiles are deployed in a random, meandering pattern. "The installation is more stone-like than mosaic-like," says Kuna.

"We needed a very durable material, and lots of it, for this large central gathering space," explains Kuna. "The tile we selected looks like natural stone, but better fit the budget and allows for easier maintenance."

ONE DREAM DESIGN
HEART HOSPITAL

The color white is frequently used in medical facilities to connote cleanliness. Ironically, however, white surfaces are exceedingly hard to keep sparkling clean. Worse, the resulting impression of sterility often serves to undermine a sense of warmth and comfort that is vital to the healing process.

Ceramic artist and illustrator Adam Rubenstein aspired to banish bland whites at the Heart Hospital in Rancho Mirage, California. Specializing in cardiac treatments, the facility's intensive-care wing features 12 private recovery suites for patients, whose recuperation can last days or even weeks. Rubenstein's design, which marries the luxury of a hotel suite with the high-tech efficiency of an operatory, features bright jolts of color chosen to uplift the human spirit.

The decorative scheme centers on ceramic-tiled floors animated with energetic shapes in punchy hues, and framed by dramatic black borders. Each room is unique: one features a checkerboard crescent that slices into a curlicue spiral, another a ribbon of red and grey that unfurls like a just-opened Christmas gift. The geometries, says Rubenstein, had diverse inspirations—from the op-art eye-teasers of M.C. Escher to Islamic motifs.

The graphics are parroted in other design elements. The abstract patterns are sandblasted into sliding-glass doors separating rooms from the circulation corridor. Matching color schemes were selected for plastic-laminate cabinets that hide critical-care equipment. Rubenstein also wrapped ceramic tile up the bathroom walls, further letting loose with patterning. Avoiding intricate mosaic-style cuts in favor of simple lines and arcing curves, Rubenstein minimized installation costs while maximizing large-scale graphic impact.

Rubenstein chose Ricchetti tile over alternatives like carpeting or linoleum due to the material's superior cleanabilty, intense coloration, and inherent resistance to germs. Tiles are set in a sealed-epoxy grout that's impervious to fluids, helping to further minimize hospital-acquired illnesses—a particular risk to intensive-care patients.

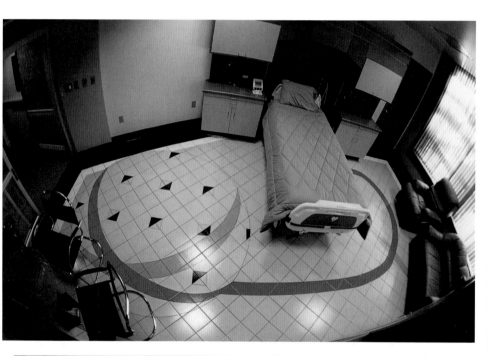

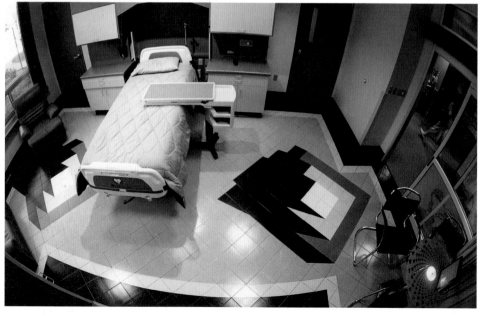

07_HOSPITALITY

The cozy Italian restaurant down the block. The hip new nightclub generating Page-Six buzz. The boutique hotel everyone's jetting to. We eat there. We drink there. We meet and greet there, and we sleep there. Hospitality projects are many and varied, but all aspire to the same goal: evoking a memorable sense of place.

The success of any hospitality venture hinges on creating wow-factor through impactful design and sustaining it through exemplary service. Designers accomplish this via environmental manipulations both subtle and bold: conjuring a home-away-from-home feel for a luxury hotel, crafting a regional flavor for a tourist-targeted restaurant, evoking an exotic location for a destination resort.

The project type puts a premium on what's original and current. Designers often use hospitality environments as a testing ground for new treatments, or to stretch traditional applications of conventional building materials. With a constant stream of innovative introductions, Italian ceramic tile manufacturers continue to be the industry's top choice for hospitality.

HIRSCH BEDNER
WESTIN RIO MAR RESORT

"With destination hospitality, guests tend to stay for long visits—
sometimes even weeks—so it's important to offer them a variety of
amenities and experiences," explains project manager Holly Kappes. The
Westin Rio Mar Beach Resort in Rio Grande, Puerto Rico, does just that,
encouraging long-term visits with two golf courses, 13 tennis courts, 10
dining venues, a pool, spa, health club, casino...the list goes on.
And so does the sprawling complex, which extends languorously along
its multi-acre oceanfront site. To make the resort feel varied but still
continuous, HBA deployed a glazed ceramic tile floor throughout a
majority of the public areas, in a terra-cotta look that evokes the
island's local heritage. "It weaves the entire property together, and
really sets the atmosphere," says Kappes.

Tile from Atlas Concorde anchors lobby areas, the ballroom prefunction space, an exterior terrace overlooking the ocean, and defines
circulation. "Where you have high traffic, there's nothing like tile," says
Kappes. "It's easier to install and maintain, and looks better over the
long run." Deployed in a checkerboard pattern, the flooring is accented
with tumbled-marble borders and inset with "area rugs" of different
tiles. "We used a range of textures and colors to keep it from looking
too monotonous," says Kappes. "In restaurants, for instance, we pulled
in more colorful tiles for walls and floors that reflect the island's
Caribbean influence." And in guestroom baths, the designers used
larger format for variety—and for maintenance: Fewer grout joints
equal enhanced cleanability.

"The Italian tiles offer the best textures, providing slip resistance
without an institutional look," says Kappes. She also praises Italian
artistry. "They are so far ahead of everyone else. They're so good at
knocking off Mother Nature that I often can't tell if a tile is ceramic
until I turn it over and read the label."

STUDIO G
BACCHUS LOUNGE

The bar-going crowd is a fickle bunch, always thirsting for the next hot destination. But it's no secret that profit and longevity are fueled by repeat customers. The recipe for success? Balancing novelty and familiarity.

A sophisticated Chicago watering hole, Bacchus Lounge does exactly that, housing a series of intimate bars—one for every mood imaginable—in a three-story space. It's possible to drink in the décor night after night and have a new experience each time. "To give customers a lot of variety, we made all three floors different, so each becomes its own destination," explains designer Gordana Jordanovska.

On the lounge's double-height second level, Jordanovska fashioned a bar surfaced entirely in Sicis glass mosaic. Starting at the ceiling plane, a swath of tile in a deep, ponderous blue drapes down along the back wall and sweeps up along the barfront. "It's like an open oyster, shiny and very sculptural," says Jordanovska. "The price point of the tile was very reasonable, which provided the opportunity to go crazy with all this gorgeous material."

Other finishes were chosen to play off the tile's texture and coloration: elliptical high-back booths upholstered in rich blue velvet, a bartop of rich mahogany. Lighting was equally important. Backlit resin panels and custom sconces in glass and copper cast a warm, enigmatic glow. A fiber-optic wall treatment cycles through a rainbow of colors. "Tile is such a beautiful material—I wanted to make sure it was visible," says Jordanovska.

She is quick to raise a glass to ceramic tile, which she often uses in hospitality settings. The trick, she says, is brainstorming new applications each time, and staying current with product introductions. "It's important to innovate, both for the public—which is increasingly sophisticated in recognizing materials and finishes—and for the designer. We're always hungry for what's new and exciting."

BARBARA LAZAROFF
WOLFGANG PUCK CAFES

Courtesy of her background in acting and set dressing, designer Barbara Lazaroff knows how to grab her audience's attention. She also knows a thing or two about making curtain calls and producing long-running hits. With former husband and business partner Wolfgang Puck, Lazaroff has grabbed the spotlight again and again with imaginative, scene-stealing restaurant interiors, starting with Los Angeles celebrity magnet Spago in 1982. Over the years, the couple has expanded its empire to include cookbooks and TV shows, as well as a bevy of upscale eateries and express-food franchises.

One of the duo's most recent productions is Wolfgang Puck Cafés, a series of cafeteria-style casual-dining establishments with nine locations and counting nationwide. The design bears Lazaroff's distinctive imprint, including an open, exhibition-style kitchen—elevating cooking to the realm of performance art—and the utterly theatrical use of ceramic tile.

Tile forms an integral part of the Wolfgang Puck Café brand identity. The signature look, easily adaptable from location to location, was sparked by the colorful company logo. Walls and floors are awash in a spirited mosaic of tile fragments. Bold strokes of black make a dramatic counterpoint to a confetti of white, red, blue, yellow, and green. Diners become submerged in a sea of tile: the material covers structural columns, frames mirrors, embellishes triangular glass sconces, and even enlivens café street fronts.

A theater maven to the core, Lazaroff has learned by experience that performance matters even more than appearance. Designers must consider lighting, ventilation, acoustics, layout—and materials that can withstand the boisterous and often messy activities of cooking, serving, and eating. As easy to maintain as it is easy on the eye, tile is truly a star vehicle in restaurant interiors.

08_EXHIBITION DESIGN

Trade shows can overwhelm even the most eager, intrepid, and receptive audience. It's easy to get lost in a barrage of ideas, absorbing little more than the sheer volume of products being proffered. The exhibition designer is charged with conceiving booths and displays that succinctly communicate a wealth of information within limited confines to crowds of people, all the while competing against other exhibitors for attention. To complicate matters, displays often travel to multiple venues; ease of set-up, de-installation, are important design criteria.

Ceramic Tiles of Italy has commissioned a number of high-profile talents to conceive temporary exhibits for tradeshows. Designers were challenged to create temporary kiosks that demonstrate the material's breadth of applications and offerings in a manner that excites, motivates, and inspires attendees. The result? Show-stopping designs for a product that truly stands out from the crowd.

ARQUITECTONICA
INTERNATIONAL TILE EXHIBITION

The design firm behind the high-rises featured in Miami Vice's opening credits, Arquitectonica has never shied away from its Florida roots. But at the 1991 International Tile Exposition, they took hometown pride to a new level with a celebration of Floridiana: a bacchanal-worthy riot of tropical fruit, palm trees, sea shells, and sizzling color.

Visitors cross a plaza of sand-toned tiles inset with dark-grey patterns conceived as illusory shadows cast by palm trees flanking the entrance. Beyond a rough-hewn mosaic-edged portal in the shape of a pineapple, glossy blue tiles wind through the zig-zag floor plan. Walls and floors feature orderly arrangements of colored tiles accented by glass mosaics—a scallop shell, a sunken pool that takes the form of a parrot. At rear, hand-crafted wrought-iron chairs and tables edged in mosaic tile invite guests to kick back and take in the tropical view.

TIGERMAN McCURRY
INTERNATIONAL TILE EXHIBITION/NEOCON

A sloping hillside town inspired Stanley Tigerman's 1992 installation for the International Tile Exhibition and NeoCon®. "I drew on the spirit of Mediterranean villages, which took shape by following the flow of the topography rather than suppressing it in the classical Roman tradition," explains Tigerman. "The urban form is organic, even incidental."

As is the exhibit, which unspools in a series of mini-buildings showcasing different manufacturers' lines. Spiraling in a freewheeling fashion around a backlit canvas enclosure housing a plein-air trattoria, the structures present surprises at every turn. Each suggests a different building type from the iconic to the symbolic and features a unique tile treatment. Peppered with tile-clad cubes that double as seating, the meandering layout is anchored by a warm grid of terra-cotta underfoot.

"Mediterranean architecture is more emotional, less intellectual, in its use of form and color," says Tigerman. "This exhibit likewise is about conveying emotion through the built environment."

AISLE
3200

ALDO ROSSI
INTERNATIONAL TILE & STONE EXHIBITION

Aldo Rossi's 1993 IT&SE booth exhibits the Pritzker Prize–winning architect's signature adherence to severe, almost reductive geometry and his postmodernist play of scale and form. Following the epigrammatic lines of classical Italian architecture, the installation takes the shape of a terra-cotta-floored piazza. Standing sentinel along the exhibit's entrance, posing like graceful four-legged beasts, is a series of peak-roofed pavilions covered in crisp tiled stripes of blue and white. Within, an energetic palette of yellow, aqua, and green tiles— introductions by some 12 Italian manufacturers—makes a multicolored nod to the show's fun-in-the-sun Miami location. The exhibition's centerpiece is a mosaic-tiled fountain that burbles invitingly, luring visitors towards the rear trattoria. Housed in a mini-palazzo complete with windows, the eatery is strewn with tables tiled in a range of schemes—one for every design appetite.

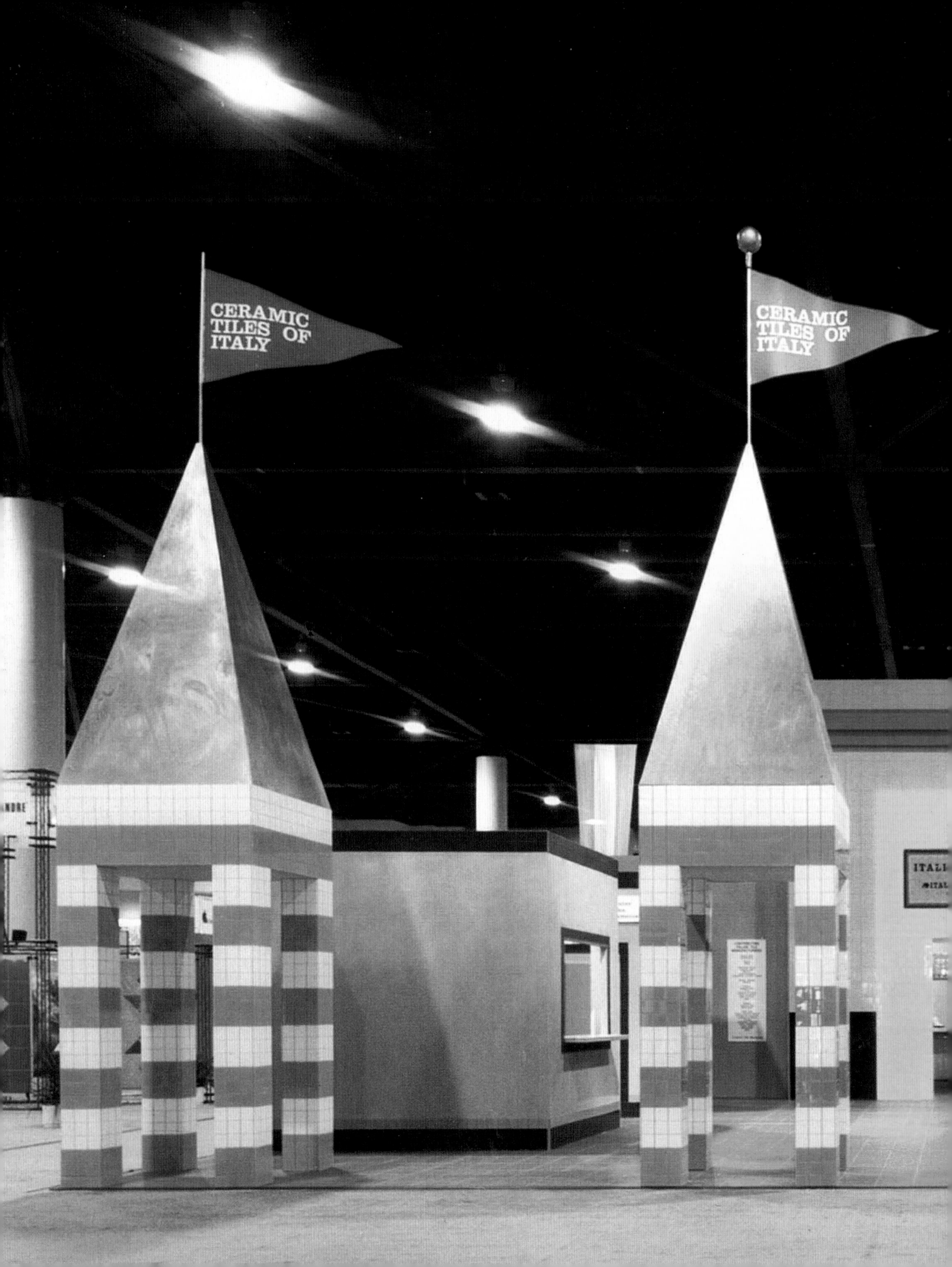
CERAMIC TILES OF ITALY
CERAMIC TILES OF ITALY

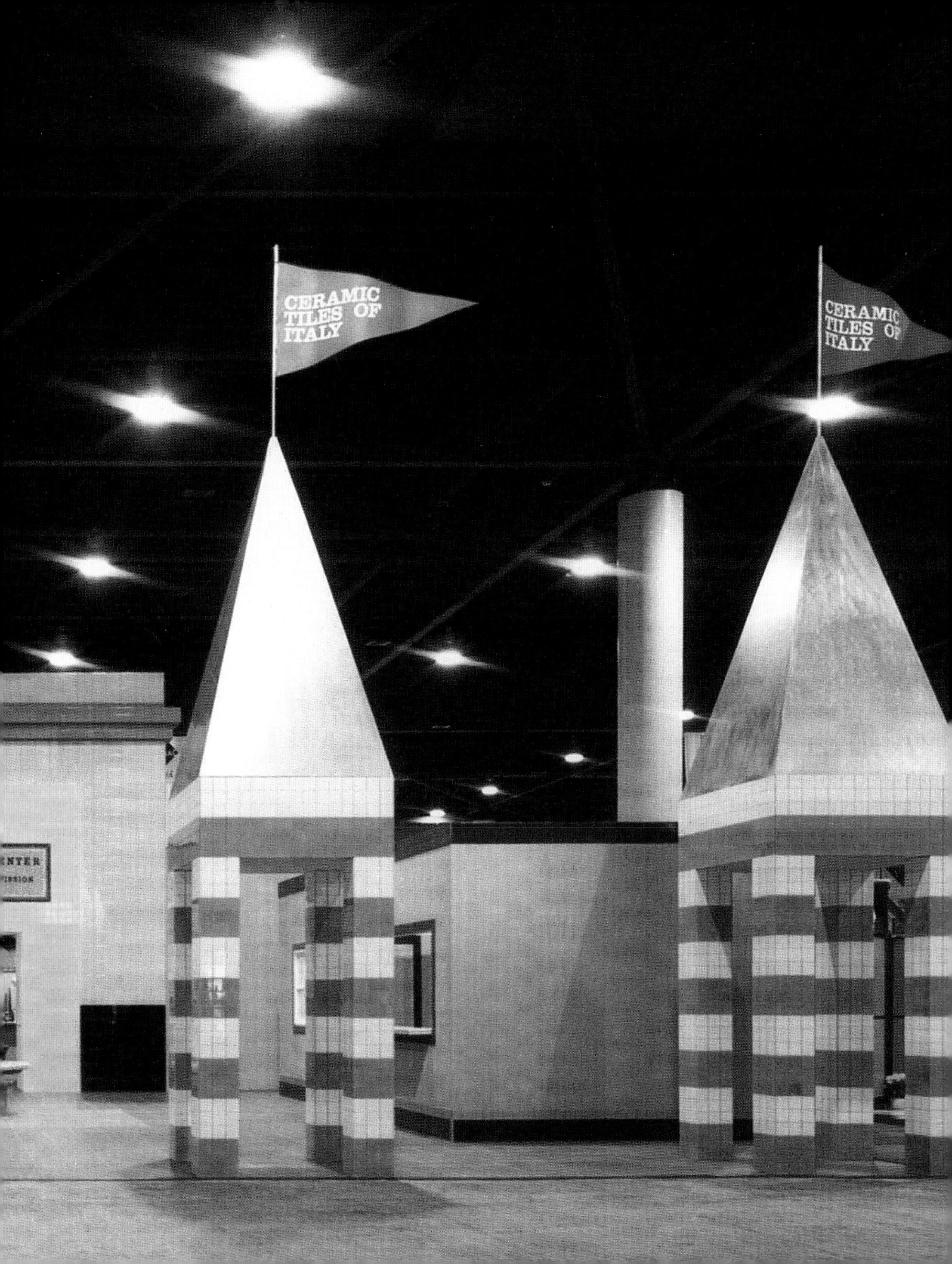

CERAMIC
TILES OF
ITALY
CERAMIC
TILES OF
ITALY

JAMES WINES/SITE
INTERNATIONAL TILE & STONE
EXHIBITION

The natural and the manmade artfully dovetail in SITE's 1994
ITSE exhibit. Dividing the booth into a welcoming front piazza
and a private rear consultation area is a boxy tile-backed
terrarium, planted by multi-tasking project architect Joshua
Weinstein. "We fused architecture and landscape to
communicate that tile is a product of the earth," says the
designer.

Cleverly telegraphing ceramic tile's diverse color options—
even those not found in nature—the terrarium's backdrop is
surfaced in a rainbow of 8-inch squares. By juxtaposing high-
contrast hues—violet against yellow, red against blue—in a
pixilated pattern, the plane appears to flicker and vibrate.
Fronting the terrarium is a glazed wall embellished with a
scattering of tiles, increasingly diffuse towards the bottom. The
complex interplay between layers of color imbues flat surfaces
with three-dimensionality, creating a tantalizing sense of depth.

GAETANO PESCE
INTERPLAN

Architect Gaetano Pesce is renowned for embracing new
materials (resins, gels, polyurethane foam) in his sometimes
radical—and always expressive—designs. But he proves just as
adept when it comes to traditional, age-old building materials.
Take tile, for instance. Commissioned to create Ceramic Tiles of
Italy's 1997 booth for the Interplan trade show, Pesce fashioned
a succinct yet whimsical solution to accommodate spatial and
economic constraints. "The budget was very small. We had to
do something simple and functional, with little detailing, but
that was still fresh," explains Pesce. And at a mere 100 square
feet, he continues, "this was perhaps the smallest project I've
done in my career!"

   Thankfully, Pesce knows how to pack a big punch in a
small package—for proof, look no further than his iconic UP
collection of vacuum-packed furniture, designed in the '60s.
Within the booth's snug 10-by-10-foot confines, Pesce created
an information-distribution station defined by exuberant wood
partitions embellished with red, white, and green tiles in the
familiar boot-shape of Italy. "I wanted the design to relate to
certain qualities of Italy—particularly its tradition of working
with clay so innovatively."

   Pesce made the most of the limited space by deploying a
grid of different floor tiles, from a black-and-white
checkerboard to a variety featuring blue scrollwork on a beige
field. "It's like a three-dimensional catalogue in the space," he
says.

   Despite Pesce's love of and experimentations in various
synthetics, sometimes, he says, only ceramic tile will do. "It's so
strong and so durable. For certain uses and applications, you
cannot exceed it with any other material."

MAUK DESIGN
CERSAIE EXHIBIT

Ceramic tile weathers all the elements with aplomb: earth, wind, water, and sun. The very same ingredients, not coincidentally, that tile is made from. Mitchell Mauk's 2001 Cersaie info-point booth celebrates tile's constituent parts with a series of totemic forms.

Representing water are carved-foam sculptures, like bubbling fountains caught in freeze-frame, surfaced in blue mosaics. Fire bursts to life in a succession of brilliant red mosaiced flames, capped by delicate gold-leafed tiles. And representing earth is a glass-fronted wall of acrylic tubes encasing powdered pigments in a spectrum of hues. To surface the tops of information stations, Mauk used translucent tiles, backlit and set below glass. "We primarily focused the tile on vertical surfaces, creating unique forms that you wouldn't normally find executed with the materials," says Mauk. "They really showcase the immaculate quality of the fabrication."

MAUK DESIGN
AIA EXHIBIT

Mitchell Mauk was challenged to brainstorm a cost-effective booth for the 2001 AIA National Convention, one that wouldn't require shipping massive amounts of heavy tile across the globe. After weighing many options, he devised an economical solution that channels the formal architecture of ancient Rome. Defining the booth's outer limits, a row of pyramid-shaped fabric-wrapped pendant lights descend like an enfilade of columns, spotlighting individual tiles below. "By placing them in a jewel-like, sculptural setting, we treated the tile as fine art—which many of them are," says Mauk. The designer scoured a vast assortment of offerings to curate his 10 personal favorites. "It was like being a kid in a candy store!"

All design elements—lights, display stands, and flooring of snap-together anti-fatigue plastic matt tiles—are drenched in fire-engine red symbolizing the Italian flag. The saturated hue also recalls another Italian icon: Ferrari, a company that's always charging full speed ahead. Just like the country's tile industry.

"All three designs for the client were implemented exactly as designed, which is the function of a very enlightened client. This kind of stuff doesn't happen in a vacuum. They really gave us the freedom, encouragement, and support to bring these ideas to fruition."

MAUK DESIGN
COVERINGS EXHIBIT

Visitors to the Coverings 2002 booth were invited to drink in Italy's most popular cultural exports—ceramic tile and, of course, cappuccino. A ribbon-like partition of transparent corrugated plastic enfolds a coffee bar and 120-seat dining area, offering welcome respite from the chaotic show floor.

Mitchell Mauk's tranquil design also addresses visual oversaturation. Rather than a comprehensive dog-and-pony show of product, Mauk showcased only one color—white—and limited tile to the floor plane. "We created a very neutral, aesthetically quiet space to stand out in sea of anarchy," he explains. The less-is-more installation, offset by slim birch planks, showcases subtle differences in shades, textures, and levels of gloss.

Displayed along the perimeter of the booth, cupped by curves in the serpentine partition, are motorized tile sculptures that spin like barbershop poles. "They're very hypnotic," says Mauk. "We wanted to bring a sense of movement into the display, since tile is usually presented as a static product."

CERAMIC TILES OF ITALY
DESIGN COMPETITION
WINNERS

1994   Barbara Lazaroff, Los Angeles, CA

1995   Tigerman McCurry Architects, Chicago, IL www.tigerman-mccurry.com

1996   Arquitectonica, Miami, FL www.arquitectonica.com

1997   Hirsch-Bedner, Santa Monica, CA www.hbadesign.com

1998   TVS & Associates, Atlanta, GA www.tvsa.com

1999   One Dream Design, Palm Springs, CA www.onedreamdesign.com

2000   Anthony Belluschi Architects, Chicago, IL www.belluschi-owpp.com

2001   Michael P. Johnson, Cave Creek, AZ www.mpjstudio.com
       Mojo Stumer, Greenvale, NY www.mojostumer.com

2002   KA, Inc., Cleveland, OH www.kainc.com
       Waddell+Associates, Lakewood, OH www.wadellarchitects.com
       Studio G, Chicago, IL www.Studio-G.net

2003   Richard Fleischman+Partners, Inc., Cleveland, OH www.studiorfa.com
       Swanke Hayden Connell, New York, NY www.shca.com
       Hemmler+Camayd, Scranton, PA www.hc-architects.com

For a complete list of Ceramic Tiles of Italy tile manufacturers
and their products visit www.italiatiles.com